Contents

Flash!

Ow! My eyes! A bright light can give you a fright – like when a camera flashes at you, or someone switches on your light on a dark winter morning. Light can also hurt you – it can damage your eyes and your skin. We are very sensitive to bright light – yet there are some types of light we can't see at all!

Light and sight

Too much light can be a pain, but most of the time, it's very useful. There's light all around us, shining from the Sun, the stars, streetlights and other light sources. It bounces off most other objects too. So we can detect all kinds of things around us by sensing light with our eyes. From the tip of your own nose, to the screen on your phone, to a star billions of kilometres away – as long as light is coming from them somehow (and your eyes are working) you can see them all.

Argh! Bright light!

What IS light?

You know light when you see it... but what is it actually made of? Light is a form of energy that shines out from burning or glowing objects. We don't see it moving as it goes so fast, but it travels along in the form of tiny energy waves called light rays. This picture shows how they move.

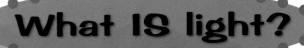

4

DISGUSTING & DREADFUL SCIENCE

Glaring Light

and other eye-burning rays

by Anna Claybourne

This edition published 2014 by Franklin Watts

Copyright © Franklin Watts 2014

Franklin Watts
338 Euston Road
London NW1 3BH

Franklin Watts Australia
Level 17/207 Kent Street,
Sydney, NSW 2000

Produced by Penny Worms & Graham Rich, Book Packagers

A CIP catalogue record for this book is available from the British Library.

Dewey Decimal Classification Number: 535

ISBN 978 1 4451 2964 8

Printed in China

Franklin Watts is a division of Hachette Children's Books, an Hachette UK company.

www.hachette.co.uk

Picture credits

Corbis images: 14t (Leah Warkentin/Design Pics); 19c (© Minnesota Historical Society). **fotolia**: 17cl (theogott). **iStockphoto.com**: title page (Dean Murray), eyeball cartoon (Elaine Barker); 7t (snipes213); 10tr (juniorbeep); 13t (Lezh); 13r (Gewoldi); 16c (pzAxe); 17b (Zitramon); 20cr and cover (mbortolino); 20bl (hakusan); 21tr (Henrik5000); 26bl (tap10); 27t (Jodi Jacobson); 27c (PlainView); 27b (craftvision). **NASA**: 5c; 9b. **Nature Picture Library**: 15b (Wild Wonders of Europe/Hodalic). **Ryan Hagerty, US Fish and Wildlife Service**: 13c. Science Photo Library: 12t (Jacopin); 24tl (Wim Van Egmond/Visuals Unlimited, Inc); 28b (Eye of Science). **Shutterstock.com**: angry monster cartoon (Yayayoyo); cover main image (Olly); 4tr (matt); 4tl (Memo Angeles); 4bl (Wichan Konchan); 5br (Zholobrov Vadim); 6t (Olga Popova); 6b (Valeriy Lebedev); 7c (Luca Flor); 8b (MarchCattle); 9t (perensanz); 10cl (copperman); 10c (Architecte®); 11tr (Julia Mihatsch); 11cl (Quayside); 11bl (Trent Townsend); 11br (Panachai Cherdchucheep); 12c (billyhoiler); 12b (Anneka); 15t (Andreas Koeberl); 15c (Simonalvinge); 17t (Augusto Cabral); 18t (Lasse Kristensen; 18b and back cover (Chianuri); 19t (Shane Gross); 20t (advent); 22t (yxowert); 22cl (Alex Kalmbach); 23tl (Anteromite); 23ctl (Katarzyna Mazurowska); 23tr (Geoffrey Jones); 23cr (Arnoud Quanjer); 23cb (Vadim Kozlovsky); 24cr (Cathy Keifer); 24b and back cover (Julia Mihatsch); 25t (Riegsecker); 25c (David Carillet); 26t (Javier Brosch); 28tl (Petr Bukal); 28tr (Dmitry Kalinovsky); 29tl (Sergej Khakimullin); 29tr (Fox Pictures); 29b and cover (DM7). **Wikipedia**: 16tr; 17cr and 26cr (Sir Godfrey Kneller); 21c (Samir).

All other illustrations by Graham Rich

Every attempt has been made to clear copyright. Should there be any inadvertent omission, please apply to the publisher for rectification.

Light forms

Light isn't just the bright rays that we can see. It comes in many forms and has some amazing qualities. X-rays, radio waves and microwaves are all types of light. In its different forms, light can cut through metal, zap zits, make hidden bloodstains glow, sizzle your skin and slice into your eyeballs! It zooms faster than a speeding bullet (about 300,000 times faster!) and even lets us look back in time...

The Earth from space, showing artificial lights (orange), sunlight (white) and the Northern Lights (green).

Wearing sunglasses and wide-brimmed hats in bright sunlight is not just about glamour – it's also good sense! They protect your eyes and skin from harmful rays.

Ouch!

Bright light is painful because your eyes contain special light-detecting cells. They have to be very sensitive so that you can see in dim light. Very strong light can overload and damage them. If this happens, your eye sends pain signals to your brain to make you shut your eyes as soon as possible.

Stre-e-etch yourself!

When you look at yourself in a spoon, a bendy fairground mirror or through water, you look all stretched, squashed or wonky. The same thing can happen to people's eyes when they wear thick glasses.

Lines of light

Rays of light normally travel in straight lines to our eyes. If there's nothing in the way, everything looks normal. But light can sometimes bend or change direction.

Refraction

Refraction happens when light passes out of one see-through substance, such as air, water or glass, into another. This makes the light rays change direction slightly.

That's why a straight straw can look broken when it stands in a glass of water, and your legs can look strangely short when you are standing in a swimming pool.

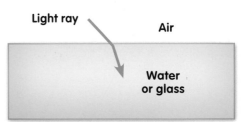

Light ray   Air

Water or glass

A curved piece of glass, like a magnifying glass lens, bends the light in different directions, making things look stretched and super-sized.

Reflection

Reflection happens when light bounces off a shiny surface like a mirror. If the mirror is flat, the light rays stay in the same pattern.

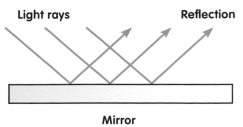

Light rays   Reflection

Mirror

If the mirror is curved or bumpy, the light rays shoot off in different directions so you see a stretched or squashed image, like the one in this bus mirror.

Stretchy shadows

As light travels in straight lines, it can't usually curve round objects. Instead, an object that isn't see-through casts a shadow – a dark area where the light rays are blocked. You can make giant shadows when the Sun is low in the sky, like the cowboy in the picture above.

See for Yourself

Casting shadows

When an object is very close to a light source, it casts a bigger shadow. Try cutting a spooky shape out of cardboard (or use your hand) and hold it near to a lamp or torch in a dark room. Can you cast funny shadows on the wall?

Time travel

Light takes time to travel across space. That means it can show us things from the past – depending on how far away it started its journey. Confused? Here's how it works.

Yikes!

If the Sun suddenly went out, we wouldn't know. We would only find out eight minutes later! But don't worry – scientists think the Sun will be around for at least another five billion years.

The speed of light

Light travels VERY fast. Its normal speed is around one billion (1,000,000,000) km/h. When you flick on your bedroom lamp, light zooms from the bulb around the room so fast, it seems instant. But in space, distances are much greater. For example, the Sun is about 150 million km away from the Earth. So light from the Sun, whizzing through space at one billion km/h, takes about eight minutes to reach us.

Look back in time...

Most things in space are even farther away than the Sun. There are stars and galaxies that are so far away, the light from them takes millions of years to reach us. And that means that we see them not now, but in the past – as they were millions of years ago. **WEIRD!**

Light travels a million times faster than a jumbo jet!

Light years

A light year is a measure of distance. It's the distance that light travels in a year. As light goes so fast, that's a long way – about 10 trillion km. That's **10,000,000,000,000** km.

OUR SUN
Our Sun is
150 million km
from Earth. It takes light
8 minutes
to reach us.
We see it as it was 8 minutes ago.

A STAR
If a star is
10 trillion km
from Earth, it takes light
1 light year
to reach us.
We see it as it was a year ago.

 See for Yourself

Yourself in the past

Even looking at yourself in a mirror means you're seeing yourself in the (very recent!) past, because of the time light takes to travel to the mirror, then back to your eyes. If you set up two mirrors facing each other, you can see lots of reflections of yourself, stretching away into the distance. Each one shows a slightly younger version of you, until they disappear.

A DISTANT STAR
If a star is
100 light years
from Earth, it takes light
100 years
to reach us.
We see it as it was 100 yeas ago.

AND SO ON...

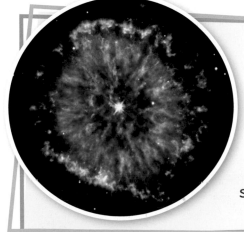

A snapshot in time

Using powerful telescopes, we can now look back into the history of the Universe. This picture, taken by NASA's Hubble Space Telescope in 2000, shows a star as it looked several thousand years ago, surrounded by a cloud ot gas.

Green slime

Dip a stick into a pond, and you're likely to pull out a trail of damp, dangly, dripping green slime. YEUCH! But what is pond slime, and why is it green? For that matter, why are most plants green? It's all to do with light.

Carbon dioxide

Sunlight

Oxygen

Water (from the roots)

Food for the rest of the plant

Plant cells under a microscope making chlorophyll.

Green energy

To live, plants need light. They use light energy from the Sun to build all their plant parts – their stems, roots, leaves, fruits and seeds – using gases from the air and water from the ground.

To do this, plants use a process called photosynthesis (meaning "making with light"). It happens inside the cells in a plant's leaves. They contain a bright green chemical called chlorophyll that can soak up sunlight and convert it to a kind of energy the plant can use.

See for Yourself

Darkness or light?

Fill two small pots with compost, and plant a couple of seeds in each. (Sunflower seeds or apple seeds are good.) Stand one pot on a sunny windowsill, and the other next to it inside a closed cardboard box. Water both plants every day. How well do they grow with and without light?

Sun grabbers

To soak up as much light as they can, the green parts of a plant spread out to catch the Sun's rays. Trees spread out their leaves wide and high. Green waterweed spreads out across ponds. Pond slime is often a mixture of water-loving plants, such as waterweed, and algae. Algae is like a plant but has no roots or leaves and it sometimes spreads out across rivers and lakes to cover the whole water surface.

Great green food machine

If it weren't for plants, we'd all starve to death! Plants use light energy to make plant parts. All those leaves, fruits and seeds provide food for plant-eating animals. Those animals get eaten by meat-eating animals. So whether you're a strict vegetarian or a burger-loving meat-muncher, you would have nothing to eat at all if it weren't for photosynthesis.

Come closer, little fly!

Yuck!

Some plants have ferocious appetites. They catch themselves extra snacks by trapping and gobbling up insects, or even frogs or mice! Pitcher plants (right) have pots with slippery slides. When animals slip in, they fall into the plant's digesting juices (like those in your tummy), which dissolve the creature so the plant can soak it up!

All about eyeballs

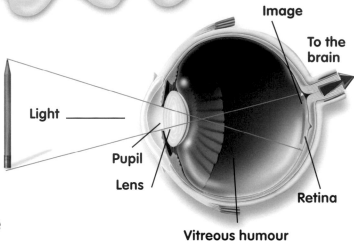

Image
To the brain
Light
Pupil
Lens
Retina
Vitreous humour

As we live on a sunlit planet, we're surrounded by light all day long. We have developed the ability to detect light, as a way of sensing our surroundings. Most animals have done the same. To collect light, we use a brilliant invention of nature – the round, squidgy eyeball.

DID YOU KNOW?

Some people find eyeballs very tasty, and eat them as a delicacy – especially fish and sheep eyes.
CHEWY!

How eyeballs work

Eyeballs are basically light-catchers. Light enters through the pupil at the front, and passes through a clear lens that bends the light rays. This casts a sharp, upside-down image onto the retina, a patch of light-detecting cells at the back of the eyeball. They turn the image into signals and send them to the brain, which flips it upright again.

Two eyes, 3D vision

Why do we have two eyes? An obvious reason is so that we can still see if we lose one. Having two eyes also means we see each object from two slightly different angles. This lets our brain work out how far away things are, giving us 3D vision. Human eyes can also distinguish about 10 million different shades of colour.

Yuck!

An eyeball has to be a hollow chamber that light can pass through for it to work. However, if it were empty, it might dry out or collapse! Instead, eyeballs are full of a gloopy but crystal-clear jelly called vitreous humour.

Eyes everywhere

Most animals have two eyes, but some have a lot more. Spiders have eight eyes – have a look at this jumping spider (left) and see if you can spot them all!

Many insects have compound eyes, made up of hundreds or even thousands of light detectors, each with its own lens. You can see them in the big bulging eyes of the fly below.

Strange eyes

The animal world has come up with some crazy-looking eye designs.

• The barreleye fish has big eyeballs that point upwards, inside its see-through head!

• A stalk-eye fly's eyes are on stalks that can be longer than its body.

• The colossal squid has the world's biggest eyeballs. They're the size of footballs!

• This caterpillar has fake eyes to scare off any creatures who may want to eat it.

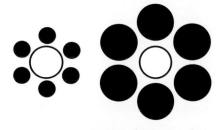

Optical illusions

Our brains sometimes get confused by the signals coming from our eyeballs. Look at this optical illusion. Which of the two white circles is bigger?

They're actually both the same.

Dark and spooky!

It's night-time, it's dark, and you can hear a strange creaking noise – heeeelp! Are you scared of the dark? Lots of people are, even adults.

Turn the light on!

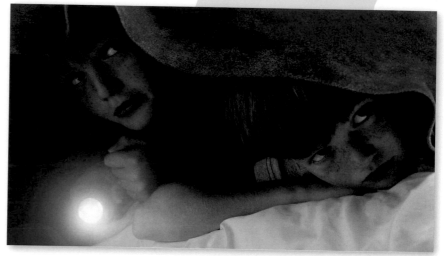

Darkness is what happens when there's no light around (or very little). Light has been important to humans since prehistoric times. We need it to see where we are and what's around us. In the dark, we feel nervous because it's harder to see any dangers nearby. Even if you know you're safe and sound in your own room, your brain can't help noticing spooky shapes in the shadows!

Life without light

Could we live without light? Besides the fact that we'd have no food (see page 11), we need sunlight. When it shines on our skin, our bodies make vitamin D, which helps us to fight off germs and keep our bones strong.

Ouch!

If you don't get enough vitamin D, you can get a horrible illness called rickets. It makes your bones painful, bendy and weak, and your teeth sore.

Too much light!

Darkness can be a good thing too. We sleep best when it's really dark. Streetlights, buildings and vehicles can cause "light pollution", meaning that in some areas it's never really truly dark. This can annoy astronomers, as they need proper darkness to view the stars. Large telescopes (right) are often located in empty deserts or on high mountains, away from city lights.

A telescope in Hawaii.

Creatures of the dark

Some animals prefer darkness. Nocturnal creatures, like moths and owls (above), usually hide during the daytime and come out at night. Some animals, known as troglobites, live in caves, where it's dark all the time. They are often blind and pale-skinned, like this strange-looking olm (below), which lives in underground rivers.

See for Yourself

Pupil play

Stand in front of a mirror in a dimly lit room. Then switch a light on and watch your eyes. Your pupils change size to take in less light when it's bright and more light when it's dark.

15

Seeing sense

Though we've always lived with light, it's taken us a long time to understand it. These brilliant scientists discovered all sorts of things about how light works.

Amazing Alhazen

Alhazen lived in Egypt around 1,000 years ago and did hundreds of experiments with light, refraction, reflection, eyes and eyesight. He found that light travels in straight lines, and showed how it enters the eye. Until then, many people thought that eyes worked by sending out invisible rays that landed on objects. Alhazen saw that it was the other way round – light rays went from objects into the eye.

Amazing!

See for Yourself

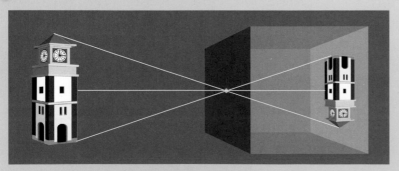

Alhazen's camera

Alhazen invented the camera obscura (or "dark room"), which works like an eyeball. Light rays enter the room through a small hole or pinhole, and create an upside-down image on the wall inside. You can make your own camera obscura in a small room on a sunny day. Make the room as dark as possible. Tape cardboard or a thick cloth over the window to completely block out the light. Make a tiny hole in the cardboard or cloth. An upside-down view of the outside world should appear on the opposite wall.

How fast is that?!

In 1638, Galileo tried to measure how fast light was. He and his assistant stood on two hilltops in the dark, flashing lanterns at each other to see how long a signal took to pass between them. Galileo decided light must travel very fast – at least 10 times faster than sound. Other scientists attempted to measure it too, but it wasn't until 1862 that Leon Foucault finally pinned down the exact speed of light (page 8). He did it using mirrors, maths and very clever measuring equipment.

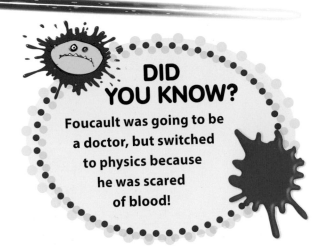

DID YOU KNOW?

Foucault was going to be a doctor, but switched to physics because he was scared of blood!

Isaac's eyeballs

Around the year 1700, Isaac Newton, one of the greatest scientists ever, also studied light. He found that shining white light through a prism, a wedge-shaped piece of glass, could bend it and split it into different colours. (The same thing happens when sunlight shines through raindrops, making a rainbow.) Newton also studied eyeballs and invented a new type of telescope.

Newton experimented with his own eyeball by sticking a bodkin (blunt needle) behind it to see if it changed his eyesight. It did...

DON'T try this at home!

I put it betwixt my eye and the bone...and pressing my eye with the end of it, there appeared several white, dark and coloured circles.

Microscopic monsters

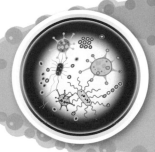

When microscopes were first invented, scientists were shocked to find tiny wriggling bacteria and creepy-crawlies living in water, soil, and even on people's teeth. UGH!

Making sparks

When it gets dark at home, you probably just flick on the electric light. Hundreds of years ago, though, lights and lamps were a bit more basic.

Yuck!

The candlefish, also called a eulachon, is a very oily, fatty ocean fish. Native Americans used to catch them, hang them up to dry, stick wicks in them, then use them as candles!

Burning bright

You can make light by setting something on fire. Burning is a kind of chemical reaction. It makes substances break down and form other substances, and this gives off energy as heat and light. Of course, if you just set fire to a stick or a piece of paper, it will soon go out, and it could be dangerous. So a long time ago, people invented lamps and candles to burn fuel more slowly and safely.

Wax and wicks

Candles can be made of many kinds of fat or wax, including beeswax or smelly whale or sheep fat. As a candle burns, the wax melts and soaks up into the stringy wick. The wax then turns into a gas or vapour in the air. The vapour burns, giving a steady light.

Oi! Leave my head alone!

Oil lamps

Simple oil lamps work in the same way as candles. They are filled with oil, which soaks into a wick, and the wick is lit at the other end. One popular kind of lamp oil came from the head of the sperm whale. People liked it because it wasn't as stinky as some other whale oils.

Early electricity

Candles and lamps with a flame were very risky. There were a lot of fires before electric lights took over. The first ever electric lamp glowed in 1809, more than 200 years ago. Scientist and inventor Humphry Davy linked a battery to a strip of carbon, making electricity flow through it. It heated up and glowed.

This photograph shows people in Minneapolis, USA, gathered to see the first illumination of electric carbon arc lamps in 1883. But carbon lamps were very smoky and smelly, so light bulbs eventually took over (see page 20).

 ## See for Yourself

Making sparks

Some materials give off a tiny bit of light when you break or tear them. Three examples are snapping or crushing a mint, such as Kendal mint cake or a polo; unrolling duct tape; or tearing open a self-adhesive envelope. Try these in complete darkness, such as under a duvet in a dark room, and you might see sparks! *

* Don't worry. These are not dangerous. They are just light sparks and won't set fire to your duvet!

Brilliant inventions

When you come up with an amazing idea – ding! – a light bulb appears above your head! (At least, it does if you're a cartoon.) The light bulb itself was a brilliant, simple idea. It changed our lives – just like many other great light-related inventions.

Who invented the light bulb?

Thomas Edison is famous for inventing the light bulb in the 1870s. In fact, several inventors came up with their own versions but Edison was the first to develop one that was easy to make, sell and use.

In a traditional light bulb, electricity flows through a tightly coiled metal filament, making it glow. The filament is inside a pear-shaped glass case, filled with a gas that helps it last longer. Today, modern inventors have come up with new types of light bulbs, like the energy-saving one on the right.

The changing shape of light bulbs over the years.

Lasers

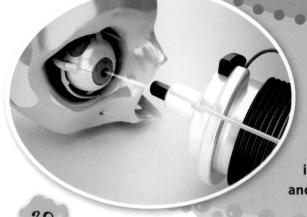

The laser, invented in 1960, is an intense, narrow beam of light that can be focused on a single point. Powerful, high-energy laser beams can cut through metal. They're also used to cut through body parts – for example in laser eye surgery, when a laser vaporises part of your eyeball to reshape it. Gentler laser beams are used in CD players, light shows, barcode scanners and to zap zits!

Cat's eyes

In 1933, Percy Shaw saw a cat's eyes shining in the night as he drove along a clifftop road, and had a great idea. His invention, the cat's eye, reflects a car's headlights so the driver can see the roadside and road markings – no batteries required! Today, there are millions of cat's eyes all over the world.

Yuck!

Doctors use fibre optic endoscopes to have a look inside people's stomachs and intestines (below). The bendy tube delivers light, so that a camera can see what's going on in there.

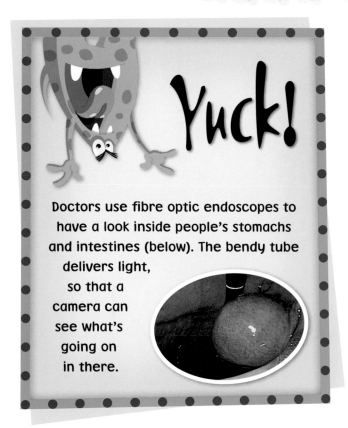

Optical fibres

Optical fibres are long, thin, bendy glass tubes. Light can travel along inside the tubes, bouncing off the inside walls, and shine out at the other end. This works even if the fibres twist, bend or go round corners. So this brilliant invention is a great way to send light from one place to another, without it having to go in straight lines. Optical fibres date from the 1840s, but are used in lots of modern inventions, like lamps and computer cables.

See for Yourself

Curving light

This experiment uses water to make a simple fibre optic tube. You need a clear plastic bottle with a small hole in the side (ask an adult to make the hole). Stand the bottle on the edge of a sink or bath, fill it with water, and shine a torch at the side opposite the hole. As water flows out of the hole, let it fall onto your hand. You should see a spot of light that has travelled through the curved water "tube".

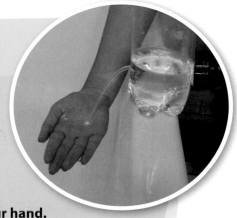

Spectrum-tacular!

We think of light as glowing and colourful – something we can see. In fact, visible light is just part of a huge range of different types of light energy – some of them frighteningly powerful. We can't see most of them, but we can detect them, and we use them for all sorts of things.

The light we can see, visible light, has medium-sized waves and is in the middle of the spectrum. Blue light has the shortest waves, ranging through the colours of the rainbow to red light, which has the longest.

The whole spectrum

The range of energy types is called the electromagnetic spectrum. You can see a diagram of it below.

Light energy travels in waves, and the different types have different wavelengths. That means the length of each wave, from the crest (top) of one to the crest of the next.

We use radio waves to carry signals long distances.

ELF/VLF are sometimes used for signal broadcasting.

Extremely Low Frequency (ELF)	Very Low Frequency (VLF)	Radio waves (short waves)	Microwaves	Infrared radiation	Visible light	Ultraviolet radiation	X-rays	Gamma rays

At this end of the spectrum, the waves are very long.

At this end of the spectrum, the waves are very short, and carry lots of energy.

Microwaves heat things up, so we use them in microwave ovens.

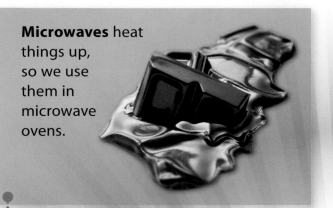

Hot things give off **infrared light**. We can detect them with special cameras.

X-rays shine through many substances, and help us take pictures of our insides.

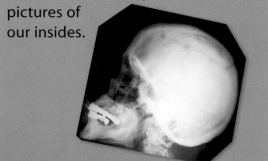

Gamma rays are powerful energy rays that come from some types of materials. They can kill germs but they can also cause severe sickness.

Signs like this warn you when there's a high risk from exposure to deadly radiation.

DID YOU KNOW?

Blood glows under ultraviolet light. At murder scenes, UV light is used to detect the faintest smears and fingerprints that might be left even after the killer has tried to clean them up.

Ultraviolet light is invisible to us, but some animals, like scorpions, glow when it shines on them! No one has yet found out why.

Yikes!

Being hit by gamma rays can cause vomiting and diarrhoea, make your hair fall out, burn your skin – and that's just a small amount. A big dose can be deadly!

23

Glowing beasts

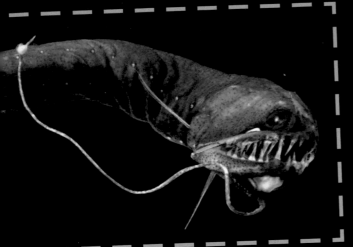

I magine having your own glowing lights built into your body! Some animals really do have this, thanks to bioluminescence (which means "living light"). They use their lights to help them see in the dark, send each other messages, lure prey or help with camouflage.

Dragon in the depths

Deep down in the sea, sunlight can't reach through the water, so it's very dark. Sea creatures that live down here often have glowing lights on their bodies. The scaleless black dragonfish (above) is one. It has tiny spotlights on its body, and bigger lights on the end of long tendrils. Scientists think these attract prey, which the dragonfish then snaps up.

Anyone want a date?

Brilliant bugs

Fireflies are creepy-crawlies with bright glowing tails. They're not actually flies, but a type of beetle. The adults glow to find each other when they fly out at night, looking for a mate. Some can even flash on and off to send messages.

Many other sea creatures including some sharks, squid and jellyfish also have glowing lights.

How it works

Bioluminescence happens when special types of chemicals combine inside an animal's body. They cause a chemical reaction that gives off light. Some creatures, like the Hawaiian squid, don't actually make their own light – instead, they have glowing bacteria living inside their bodies. The bacteria make the light, acting like a lantern for the squid. In return, the squid feeds the bacteria and offers them a safe place to live.

Yikes!

In marshy, boggy places, you can sometimes see strange, flickering lights hovering around at night. People used to think they were ghosts or fairies, and called them "Will o' the wisps" or "spook lights". In fact, they come from gases bubbling up from the bog, mixing together, and catching fire.

Cats' eyes

At night, cats' eyes (above) seem to glow. However, they are not bioluminescent – they don't give out light, only reflect it. Cats, along with tigers, sharks, owls and many other animals, have a silvery layer (like a mirror) at the back of each eye that reflects light. This makes the light hit the eye's light-detecting cells twice instead of once, helping cats to see well in the dark.

25

Deadly light

Light gives us life, but too much of it in the wrong place or at the wrong time can be a serious problem. It can even be a killer – so beware!

Sizzling in the Sun

You probably know you should cover up your skin in the sunshine, or wear plenty of suncream. That's because the Sun's rays include ultraviolet light that can burn skin badly. Sunburn turns those with pale, sensitive skin bright red and makes it feel sore, blister and peel off in flakes.

Not one of my better ideas...

Don't look!

You should never look directly at the Sun. Isaac Newton, not content with poking himself in the eye (see page 17), tried covering one eye and staring at the Sun for several minutes with the other. The vision in this eye began changing colour, and was filled with spots and blobs. Newton had to rest in a dark room for several days before he could see properly again, and his eye was probably damaged for life.

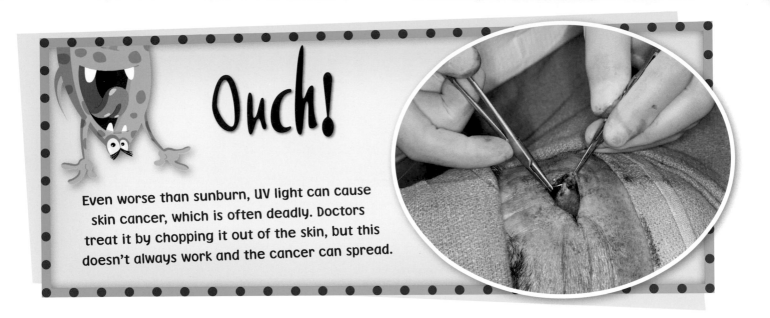

Ouch!

Even worse than sunburn, UV light can cause skin cancer, which is often deadly. Doctors treat it by chopping it out of the skin, but this doesn't always work and the cancer can spread.

Aaaarrrggh! My eyes!

Bright light can also cause headaches and temporary blindness, and has even been used as a method of torture. Polar and mountain explorers often wear snow goggles to cut out the glare of sunlight reflecting off the snow, as it can cause "snow blindness". Dazzling sunshine can also be hazardous for fighter pilots, so they wear helmets, like this one, with special eye shades.

Too bright for my brain

On TV, you sometimes hear a warning that flashing lights are about to appear. That's because they can be bad for people who have a brain disease called epilepsy. Photo flashes or flickering disco lights can trigger a dangerous epileptic fit, making the sufferer fall to the ground and tremble.

The future's bright

Scientists haven't finished experimenting with light – they're still working on new ways to use it, and exciting new light technologies.

Now you see me, now you don't!

At the moment, our attempts at becoming invisible are basic camouflage, such as these ones. Invisibility cloaks only exist in sci-fi stories and the pages of Harry Potter – but that is set to change. Scientists are working on ways to bend light around an object, so that it seems to disappear. One way of doing this uses optical fibres. Another idea is for a cloak or suit that videos what is going on behind it, then projects it towards the viewer.

A natural glow

Imagine a pet cat that glows in the dark! What about using glowing trees and plants instead of streetlights? Scientists have already found ways to copy genes (instructions found in cells) from glowing creatures, such as jellyfish, and add them to other living things like mice (left), to make them give off light. The reason? So they can see that the technique has actually worked! This genetic engineering could help people in the future with all sorts of diseases and illnesses.

28

Light power

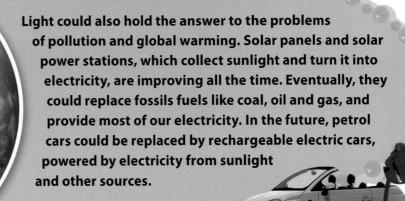

Light could also hold the answer to the problems of pollution and global warming. Solar panels and solar power stations, which collect sunlight and turn it into electricity, are improving all the time. Eventually, they could replace fossils fuels like coal, oil and gas, and provide most of our electricity. In the future, petrol cars could be replaced by rechargeable electric cars, powered by electricity from sunlight and other sources.

See for Yourself

Why are solar panels dark?

Take a sheet of black paper and a sheet of white paper, and tape them to a sunny window to soak up the sunlight. Leave them for five minutes, then test which is warmer. White surfaces reflect light and heat, while black surfaces are better at absorbing it. Solar panels are dark blue or black because it helps them to take in as much light as possible.

Laser weapons

In sci-fi films, baddies have scary laser guns. Could they really exist? Some laser weapons have actually been made, but they use a lot of power and don't work very well. One type of non-deadly laser gun is being developed to control crowds. In the future, we could certainly see more of them.

Glossary

algae simple plant-like things but without stems, roots or leaves

bacteria tiny single-celled living things

bioluminescence light given off by living things

camera obscura dark room where light enters through a tiny hole, making an upside-down image

camouflage colours and patterns that allow something to blend into the background

electromagnetic spectrum (EMS) range of different wavelengths of light energy

filament a thin thread or wire

galaxy a huge cluster or swirl of stars in space

gamma rays a type of light energy wave

genetic engineering experimenting with genes

infrared light a form of light energy that we cannot see

laser a type of of intense light in a narrow beam

lens a clear, curved object that bends light rays

light year the distance light travels in one year

optical fibre a flexible tube that light can travel along

microwave a type of light energy wave

nocturnal active at night

Northern Lights pattern of light in the sky, caused by particles from the Sun

photosynthesis the process plants use to build plant material using light energy

physics the science of forces, energy and matter

prism a wedge-shaped, clear object that splits light into colours

pupil hole in the eyeball that lets light in

reflection light bouncing off a surface

refraction light bending as it passes between different substances

retina light-detecting area at the back of the eyeball

ultraviolet (UV) light a form of light energy that we cannot see

vitreous humour clear jelly inside the eyeball

X-ray a type of light energy wave

Websites and Places to visit

Optics for Kids: Exploring the Science of Light
http://www.optics4kids.org/
Facts about light and light scientists, interesting activities and experiments, and amazing optical illusions to try.

Science Kids: Light
http://www.sciencekids.co.nz/light.html
Experiments, games, activities and fun facts all to do with the science of light.

How the eye works
http://www.childrensuniversity.
manchester.ac.uk/interactives/science/
brainandsenses/eye/
Learn more about how we use our eyes to see.

HubbleSite
http://hubblesite.org/
Find out everything you could want to know about the Hubble Space Telescope, and view some of the amazing sights it has seen.

National Media Museum
Bradford,
West Yorkshire,
BD1 1NQ, UK
http://www.nationalmediamuseum.org.uk/

Science Museum
Exhibition Road,
South Kensington,
London SW7 2DD, UK
www.sciencemuseum.org.uk

Glasgow Science Centre
50 Pacific Quay
Glasgow G51 1EA, UK
www.gsc.org.uk

Edinburgh's Camera Obscura and World of Illusions
Castlehill, The Royal Mile,
Edinburgh, EH1 2ND
www.camera-obscura.co.uk

MOSI
Museum of Science and Industry
Liverpool Road, Castlefield,
Manchester M3 4FP
http://www.mosi.org.uk

Exploratorium
Palace of Fine Arts,
3601 Lyon Street,
San Francisco, CA 94123, USA
www.exploratorium.edu

Index